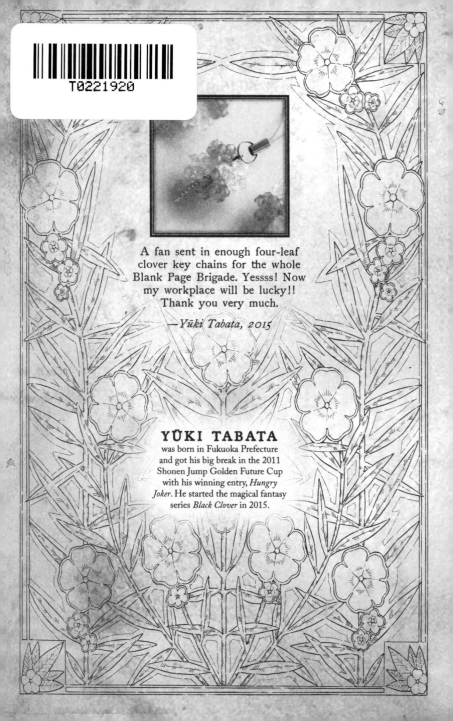

A fan sent in enough four-leaf clover key chains for the whole Blank Page Brigade. Yessss! Now my workplace will be lucky!! Thank you very much.

—Yūki Tabata, 2015

YŪKI TABATA was born in Fukuoka Prefecture and got his big break in the 2011 Shonen Jump Golden Future Cup with his winning entry, *Hungry Joker*. He started the magical fantasy series *Black Clover* in 2015.

BLACK CLOVER
VOLUME 4
SHONEN JUMP Manga Edition

Story and Art by YŪKI TABATA

Translation ✿ TAYLOR ENGEL,
HC LANGUAGE SOLUTIONS, INC.

Touch-Up Art & Lettering ✿ ANNALIESE CHRISTMAN

Design ✿ FAWN LAU

Editor ✿ ALEXIS KIRSCH

BLACK CLOVER © 2015 by Yuki Tabata
All rights reserved.
First published in Japan in 2015 by SHUEISHA Inc., Tokyo.
English translation rights arranged by SHUEISHA Inc.

The stories, characters and incidents mentioned in
this publication are entirely fictional.

Printed in Italy

Published by VIZ Media, LLC
P.O. Box 77010
San Francisco, CA 94107

10 9 8 7 6 5
First printing, December 2016
Fifth printing, March 2024

PARENTAL ADVISORY
BLACK CLOVER is rated T for Teen and is
recommended for ages 13 and up. This volume
contains realistic and fantasy violence.

VIZ MEDIA
viz.com

SHONEN JUMP

Fuegoleon

Asta

Leopold

Black✽Clover

YŪKI TABATA

4

THE CRIMSON
LION KING

Yuno

Squad: The Golden Dawn
Magic: Wind

Asta's best friend, and a good rival who's been working to become the Wizard King right alongside him since they were little.

Asta

Squad: The Black Bulls
Magic: None (Anti-Magic)

He has no magic, but he's working to become the Wizard King through sheer guts and his well-trained body.

Charmy Pappitson

Squad: The Black Bulls
Magic: Cotton

She's small, but she eats like a maniac.

Noelle Silva

Squad: The Black Bulls
Magic: Water

A royal. She's really impudent, but can be kind too.

Fuegoleon Vermillion

Squad: The Crimson Lion Kings
Magic: Flame

A captain with a strong sense of justice. He's Mimosa's cousin and Leopold's older brother.

Mimosa Vermillion

Squad: The Golden Dawn
Magic: Plant

Noelle's cousin. She's calm, gentle and a bit of an airhead.

Nozel Silva

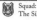

Squad:
The Silver Eagles
Magic: Mercury

A proud captain.
Noelle's older
brother.

Leopold Vermillion

Squad: The Crimson
Lion Kings
Magic: Flame

An innocent,
self-confident guy.
Mimosa's cousin
and Fuegoleon's
younger brother.

Solid Silva

Squad:
The Silver Eagles
Magic: Water

Noelle's older
brother.

Xebra Silva

Squad:
The Silver Eagles
Magic: Mist

Noelle's older sister.

???

Squad: ?
Magic: ?

A mystery man who's
launched a surprise
attack on the capital.
He has a bitter
grudge against the
Clover Kingdom…

Sol Marron

Squad: The Blue
Rose Knights
Magic: Earth

She's a carefree
Amazon, but she
adores her captain.

STORY

In a world where magic is everything, Asta and Yuno are both found abandoned on the same day at a church in the remote village of Hage. Both dream of becoming the Wizard King, the highest of all mages, and they spend their days working toward that dream.

The year they turn 15, both receive grimoires, magic books that amplify their bearer's magic. They take the entrance exam for the Magic Knights, nine groups of mages under the direct control of the Wizard King. Yuno, whose magic is strong, joins the Golden Dawn, an elite group, while Asta, who has no magic at all, joins the Black Bulls, a group of misfits. With this, the two finally take their first step toward becoming the Wizard King…

In light of their conquest of the dungeon, Asta and the others are invited to be guests at the distinguished service ceremony, held for Magic Knights who achieve things. However, they find themselves in a tense standoff with the assembled veterans from each brigade! They then receive word that the royal capital is under attack. Asta and the others leap into action to save the country from peril!

CONTENTS

BLACK ❉ CLOVER

4

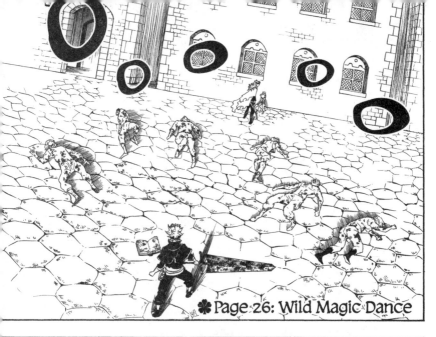

Page 26: Wild Magic Dance

GET AWAY FROM THAT GIRL, YOU CRAZY JERK!!

SO, SOMEBODY SHOWS UP...

...AND NOT ONLY IS HE FROM THE BULLS, HE'S JUST A KID!

You can't stop my army with an attack like that!!

You moron!!

HUH
?!

WAIT
...

HUSSSH

FSH

!

GEEZ,
KID, YOU
CAN
MOVE!

WHU—

I
WAS SO
SCARED!

Nobody
asked...

...for
a no-
magic
nobody
like
you!!

I GET IT!
YOU'RE THAT
ANTI-MAGIC
GUY!

SCRITCH

AAAAH...
AAARRGH
...

QUIT
MESSING
WITH ME.

West District

I THOUGHT I'D HAVE DESSERT WHEN WE GOT BACK...

...BUT THEIR LOOKS HAVE MADE ME LOSE MY APPETITE.

...

WHAT ARE THESE FIENDS...?! WE CUT THEM DOWN, AND THEY JUST GET RIGHT BACK UP!

YES, THEY ARE. JUST LOOKING AT THEM MAKES ME WANT TO VOMIT.

THESE GUYS ARE SERIOUSLY CREEPY, SIS!

East District

North-west District

DO THEY HAVE SOME SORT OF WEAKNESS?

LOOKING FOR IT WOULD TAKE TOO MUCH TIME!

THERE ARE SO MANY OF THEM!

...BUT THEY'RE NOT LIVING HUMANS!

THESE THINGS... THERE'S MAGIC IN THEM...

North District

IN THAT CASE...

PUNISHMENT FOR THE CRIME OF DARING TO THREATEN THE PEOPLE...

...OF THIS COUNTRY.

ANYONE WHO'S INJURED, COME TO ME!

WHAT AWESOME MAGIC!!

THAT'S THE MAGIC KNIGHTS FOR YOU!!

THEY'RE FANTAS-TIC!!

MY MAGIC RUNS MY OWN MANA THROUGH CORPSES, MAKING THEM MOVE ANY WAY I WANT.

IT'S WRAITH MAGIC!

THAT GUY'S ATTACKS...

THEY INSTANTLY CUT THROUGH THE MANA IN THE CORPSES, ERASING IT!!

WHY ARE YOU ATTACKING INNOCENT PEOPLE, YOU SLEAZEBAG?!

WHY?

I'M GONNA TAKE YOU DOWN!!

VSH

IRK

BOOMF!

"Innocent"
...?

M

BLORP

BLORP

GRU NGH

FWOOSH

NUMBER FOUR... JIMMY!

...

The Assorted Questions Brigade

Good day! Good evening! Good morning!
Here it is, the first question corner.
I'm so relieved we got lots of letters.
Please keep giving us your support!!

✾

Q: Which character do you have the most fun drawing? (Dragon, Tokyo)

A: The one who's most fun to draw is Charmy! She moves around in fun ways. So I guess Asta's fun too.

Q: What's the difference between magic power and mana? (Human with Absolutely No Magic, Kanagawa)

A: Mana is something fundamental and invisible that floats in the air. When mana makes its home in a living creature, it turns into power that can influence other substances, and that's magic power. When magic power is refined even further, it becomes magic... I think that's how it goes. I'm sorry I can't explain it better.

Q: How many members are in the Black Bulls? Also, is the Black Bulls member who says "FSSHHH" TV personality Matsuko Deluxe? (Kouhei Yamada, Fukushima)

A: They've got about a dozen members, I think. Lots of them are free spirits, so I'm not really sure...
The "FSSHHH" person is... There might be a hint in the back of this volume!!

THAT'S NOT FAIR, YOU JERK!

YOU'VE BEEN BRINGING OUT ALL KINDS OF CREEPY STUFF!

THAT BRAT'S YOUR PREY THIS TIME AROUND...

JIMMY!

JIMMY JUST GOT YOU WITH HIS SPECIAL-MADE CURSE SHELL. IT'S LOADED UP WITH CURSE POWER!

EVEN SCRATCHES WON'T STOP BLEEDING NOW.

BA-DMP BA-DMP

SSS SSS

...

I'M BLEEDING.....

I WON'T BE ABLE TO SWING THE BIG SWORD FAST ENOUGH!!

I'd be real careful if I were you!

BA BA BA BA

RAAAAH!!

BAM

FOR A BRAT WITH NO MAGIC, YOU'RE KIND OF A PAIN...

JIMMY'S STILL GOT LOTS OF CURSE POWER LEFT THOUGH.

BUT... FIRST...

VV M V M

HUH...?

VUMMm

Jimmy! Finish off the brat in the back! She's an eyesore!!

YOU KNIGHTS PROTECT THE PEOPLE, HUH...

AHH, AHH, THAT'S RIGHT.

SCRTCH

HA HA HA

SCRTCH

WHO'RE YOU AIMING AT?!

Aim for that brat, Jimmy!!

I'LL PROTECT HER EVEN IF THERE'S NOTHING TO GAIN FROM IT!!

IRK

...and swing your sword around until you bleed to death, moron!!

You will, huh? All right, stay there ...

ASTA!

I HAVE TO HELP HIM, OR ELSE...

HOW... COULD SOMEONE LIKE ME...

...

FLINCH

YOU DO NOT BELONG HERE.

LEAVE THIS PLACE, YOU FAILURE!

GRAH

...

I'M SURPRISED YOU HAD THE NERVE TO RETURN TO THE NOBLE'S REALM!

YOU WERE PRACTICALLY EXILED FROM THE SILVAS.

RIGHT, NOELLE?!

A RECORD-BREAKING EMBARRASSMENT WHO CAN'T EVEN CONTROL HER MAGIC PROPERLY!

BLACK BULLS GIRL...

DON'T TELL ME YOU'VE LET THE THINGS YOUR SIBLINGS SAID FRIGHTEN YOU.

ONE WRONG DECISION MEANS ONE LOST LIFE!!

THERE IS NO TIME FOR SUCH THINGS ON THE BATTLE-FIELD!!

...

IF YOU JOINED THE KNIGHTS OF YOUR OWN FREE WILL...

...THEN STEEL YOURSELF AND GET STRONGER!!

YOU ARE STANDING HERE AS A MEMBER OF THE MAGIC KNIGHTS!

BEING WEAK IS NOTHING TO BE ASHAMED OF.

STAYING WEAK IS!!

ISN'T THAT WHAT HE KEEPS PROVING...?!

THAT'S RIGHT...

OH N—

Water Creation Magic: Sea Dragon's Lair!!

BABABA

Say what ....?!

NOELLE!!

HONESTLY! THAT'S JUST PAINFUL TO WATCH!

I'LL SAVE YOU, SO YOU'D BETTER BE GRATEFUL!!

WHAT ARE YOU DOING, DORKSTA?!

BAH

You little brats!!

SHUF

HEH HEH HEH

SO YOU'RE BACK IN ACTION, HUH?

IF YOU CAN MOVE FREELY, HE'LL NEVER BE ABLE TO STOP YOU. GO!!

...get cocky!!

Don't...

GET THAT MONSTER GOOD!!

SHOW ME YOUR POWER!!

BRR BRR

I'LL BACK YOU UP, RIVAL!!

THANK YOU VERY MUUUUCH!!

UMMMMMM ...

who's that guy?

And...

I WAS GONNA DO THAT ANY-WAY!

LET'S HURRY AND EVACUATE!

WHROOSH

FOOM

FOOM

HEAD CHEF, WHAT ARE YOU DOING?!

✿ Page 28: Blackout

DELIVER THE ULTIMATE DISH UNDER *ANY* CIRCUM-STANCES!! THAT'S WHAT THE BEST DO!!

YOU *FOOLS*!! AS IF A CHEF COULD ABANDON HIS COOKING RIGHT IN THE MIDDLE AND RUN!!

BAAAAAM

I'M TELLING YOU, WE NEED TO RUN—

BAH!

?!

WELL, IT'S A NATIONAL EMERGENCY, SIR!!

WHAAAAT?! LEAVING WITHOUT EATING MY MAIN COURSE?! WHAT DO THEY THINK THEY'RE DOING?!

YES, BUT THE KNIGHTS ARE ALL GONE! NOBODY'S HERE NOW!

BAAAAAM

THAT MAIN COURSE OR WHATEVER IT IS!

LET ME EAT IT, PLEEEEEASE!!!

AND BESIDES...

THAT'S A MAGIC KNIGHTS ROBE... MEANING... SHE MUST BE ONE OF THE BIG SHOTS WHO GOT INVITED TO THE DECORATION CEREMONY.

WHA...? WHO'S THE SHRIMP?

TH... THAT WAS REALLY GROSS!

BADMP BADMP

PHEW

HMPH... THAT JUST ABOUT DOES IT.

I NEED TO GET STRONGER SO THINGS LIKE THIS DON'T GIVE ME TROUBLE.

NO MATCH FOR US, AT ANY RATE.

...

WHAT WERE THOSE THINGS ANYWAY?

SOL, DON'T SAY THINGS PEOPLE WILL MISINTER-PRET.

I CAN'T BELIEVE YOU TRIED TO ATTACK MY SIS, YOU MORONS!

ONLY THE WOMEN OF THE BLUE ROSE KNIGHTS ARE ALLOWED TO TOUCH HER!

YAAAY

LONG LIVE THE MAGIC KNIGHTS!!

WHAT INCREDIBLE POWER!!

...

THAT'S ODD.

WHAT WAS THE ENEMY THINKING, UNLEASHING CREATURES THIS WEAK? WHERE IS THEIR MAIN FORCE?

HEH HEH

THAT WASN'T NEARLY FUN ENOUGH.

WA HA HA

WHAT? DONE ALREADY?!

49

IT LOOKS AS THOUGH THEY'VE ALL... ENTERED THE MARKED AREAS.

GLOW

!

SO WERE THEY REALLY AFTER... THE KING?!

BAH

A FEINT...

WHAT
...?!

ZUM

ZUM

!!

OH
NO

ZUM
ZUM

THIS
IS...

ZUM

ZUM

Spatial Magic.

WELL
DONE...

...MAGIC
KNIGHTS.

WHA
...

WHAT
IS
THAT?!

Blackout

THE MAGIC
KNIGHTS...
DISAPPEARED?

I KNEW THE ENEMY HAD A SKILLED SPATIAL-MAGIC USER... BUT I NEVER DREAMED THEY'D BE THIS GOOD!

THEY GOT US!

WE SEEM TO BE SEVERAL HUNDRED KILOMETERS AWAY FROM THE CAPITAL, AT THE VERY LEAST.

...

WHERE ARE WE?!

CURSE!!

...

ALL THOSE AMAZING MAGIC KNIGHTS FELL FOR A TRAP LIKE THAT ONE?

HOW AMAZINGLY *STUPID!*

KYA

AAAAH!

HA HA HA HA HA

Quit pretending you're cute!!

YOU SOWS!!

MY! YOU'RE KINDA HANDSOME, AREN'T YOU! ♪

AAAAAGH! ELIZA!!

YOU MONSTER!! WHAT HAVE YOU DONE?!

HOW OLD DO I LOOK??

COME ON, TELL ME! ♪

SAY, AM I PRETTY?

SO SOMEONE *DID* ESCAPE THAT SPATIAL MAGIC!

MY MY MY.

61

THOSE ARE CURSE BULLETS WITH ALL SORTS OF CURSES INSIDE!!

YOU WON'T KNOW WHAT YOU'RE GOING TO GET UNTIL THEY HIT YOU! ♪

SURE. YOU'RE HANDSOME, SO I'LL TELL YOU. ♪

MY, YOU THINK YOU CAN FIGHT AND TALK?

WHAT ARE YOU PEOPLE?

WHY DID YOU ATTACK!?

Well? And?

WHO DO YOU THINK IT IS?

!

WE'RE HERE TO ELIMINATE A CERTAIN SOMEONE!! THAT'S WHY!!

Not that I'm going to tell you!!

WHERE
...

...IS THE WIZARD KING?!

...SHOULD BE THE FIRST RESPONSIBILITY OF THE NATION'S STRONGEST MAGE!

I AM THE RULER OF THIS LAND! IN A CRISIS LIKE THIS ONE, STAYING BY MY SIDE...

REST ASSURED, YOUR MAJESTY. WE, THE ADVISERS OF THE WIZARD KING, WILL PROTECT YOU.

I AM THE ONE AND ONLY LEADER OF THIS COUNTRY!

HE'S GOTTEN FULL OF HIMSELF BECAUSE HIS AUTHORITY EQUALS MINE WHEN WE'RE AT WAR, HASN'T HE?!

ARRRRGH! WHERE DID HE GO, ANYWAY!? HE'S ALWAYS FAR TOO FREE AND EASY ABOUT THESE THINGS!!!

HA HA HA

I'M STEPPING OUT FOR A BIT. IF ANYTHING HAPPENS, HANDLE IT.

...

THE ATTACKS JUST KEEP COMING!

SHE HAS HUGE MAGIC RESERVES!

MY, MY! YOU'RE GETTING CLUMSIER AND CLUMSIER..

WHAT HIT YOU THIS TIME, I WONDER?

I CAN BARELY SEE ANY- MORE!

MY EYES...

RRGH...

...IS GOING NUMB...

!

MY BODY...

THIS IS HER POWER...

HEE HEE

...MY EARS ARE FAIL- ING!

AND NOW ...

Bit by bit... while trembling with terror...

...you'll pay dearly for calling me old.

ASH CURSE MAGIC, *CHEERFUL ASH DESTRUC-TION.*

...

...AND I WAS ADMITTED TO THE GOLDEN DAWN, THE STRONGEST GROUP THERE IS RIGHT NOW.

THE FOUR-LEAF CLOVER RAISED THEIR EXPECTA-TIONS...

...WAS I TRYING TO...

WHAT EXACTLY...

JUST WAIT. HE'LL GO UNDER SOON.

HMPH! HIS ABILITIES ARE NOTHING COMPARED TO THE REST OF THE GOLDEN DAWN.

So maybe he's got a four-leaf clover, but that peasant is pushing his luck.

I WAS ONLY HONING MY SKILLS TO KEEP FROM LOSING.

IT DIDN'T MATTER WHAT OTHER PEOPLE SAID.

...I COULDN'T WIN.

BUT...

...WAS A POWER I WAS GIVEN BY CHANCE AND CAN'T CONTROL.

WHAT DEFEATED THAT GUY...

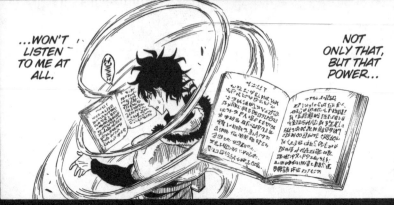

...WON'T LISTEN TO ME AT ALL.

NOT ONLY THAT, BUT THAT POWER...

BECAUSE THAT POWER, WHICH I REALLY CAN'T CALL MY OWN, REACTED.

IT'S HOW I ESCAPED FROM THAT SPATIAL MAGIC TOO.

"...FROM A PEASANT LIKE HIM."

"IT ISN'T AS IF WE'RE EXPECTING MUCH...

...THE THING THAT REALLY FRUSTRATES ME!!

THAT ISN'T...

NO... THAT'S NOT IT.

THIS IS...

...THE FLOW OF MANA...?!

It's said that mages with wind-based mana are particularly good at detecting mana.

...and then attempted to *go beyond even that.*

...showed an astonishing ability to detect mana...

With all five senses cut off and his back against the wall, Yuno, with his finely honed concentration...

I want to know all sorts of things about you! Can you hear me??

Come on, hurry, tell me!!

KYA HA HA HA HA HA HA HA HA HA

If you don't, I'll kill you right now!!

Go on, go on, hurry up! Hurry and beg for your life!

I DON'T CARE ABOUT YOU.

I JUST...

SHUT UP.

AHH...

HIM...

HUH?

THIS FEELING... THAT BOY...

THE MANA... IT'S GATHERING?!

Sylph's Breath

I WAS RELYING ON MY SIGHT AND HEARING SO MUCH THAT I COULDN'T SEE THEM.

I SEE... THIS SPIRIT HAS BEEN CONSTANTLY SENDING ME MANA SIGNS.

THIS IS BAD!!

IF I DON'T USE THE MAGIC I STOLE TO PROTECT MYSELF, THEN—

...

NOT... ENOUGH... MANA!!

YAAH

THIS IS WHY I TOLD YOU WE NEEDED TO RUN!!

WE'RE UNDER ATTACK !!

A WITCH ...

Give it to meee...

Give it to me...

I HAVE TO STEAL SOME, OR ELSE ...!

GLEAM GLEAM

LOOM

ZUM ZUM

NOOOOOOO!

Give it to meeee!

GIVE IT TO HER ...?

NUH... NOOOOOOO!

MY...MY FOOD?!

WHAT IS THAT?!

WAAAAH

!

THE FEEL OF THIS MANA... I KNEW IT! THAT WOMAN'S STILL ALIVE!

THIS GROWING, SWELLING...

Give it to meeee!

...MAGIC...

Strike
of the
Sleeping
Sheep

HOW D'YA LIKE THAT?! THE PASSION IN MY COOKING POWERED UP THAT SHRIMP'S MAGIC!!

Glad you liked it!!

Seriously?!

I WILL FOLLOW YOU MY ENTIRE LIFE, HEAD CHEF!!

TH... THAT WAS AWESOME!!!

WHOOOOAA

I DON'T CARE WHO THEY ARE— NOBODY TOUCHES MY FOOD!

FWEPH

SW SW

FOOOD!!

SW SW

TMP TMP

LAAAA!!

FFT

WHROOSH!!

FVOM

Gruuuuub!

THEN IT REALLY WAS HER...!

"Grub"?

OH! A BLACK BULLS ROBE...

BLURRR

A KID...?

Gruuub!

THAT TREMENDOUSLY STRONG MAGIC... WAS IT FROM HER?

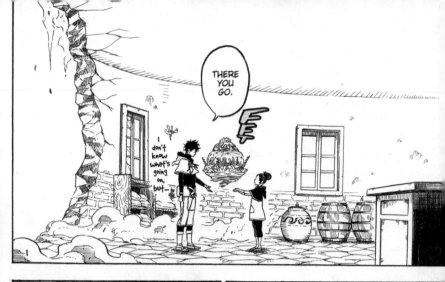

THERY
YOU
GO.

I don't know what's going on, but...

LA...ooo

?

BADMP

NO
PROB.

?

TH...
TH...

THANK
YOU
VERY
MUCH!

MY MEAL-
SAVING
PRINCE HAS
ARRIVED!

I'LL HAVE TO...GET BETTER AT USING IT...

I GUESS... THAT SPELL PUTS QUITE A STRAIN ON ME.

LA?!

WOBBLE

!

UM...UM... C-COULD I ASK YOUR NAME?

FWMP

POOF

FLIPIPIP

LOOK OUT!!

ZZZZ

POOF

LA... LAAAAA...

POOF

W-WELL... I GUESS I'D BETTER EAT THIS.

NOM NOM

RRRAAH!

SPAK
SPAK
KRAKL

KRAKL
KRAKL
WHIRR

Rrgh
...!!

NUMBER TWO... ALFRED.

SPLOOOSH

ASTA!!

IF I CAN LEND HIM MY STRENGTH, LIKE BEFORE...

Even that extra-special anti-magic sword of yours...

...is pretty pointless if your enemy's airborne and you can't touch him.

WEEN

NEEN

THE WOUNDS THAT GUY GAVE HIM EARLIER ARE...!

BRRR BAAM

That guy's your opponent!!

ASTA!! ...

THAT'S A BAD MATCH FOR ME!!

RRGH ...

MUDDY WATER MAGIC!

BOOM

A-HAHAHA

I control corpses and win just by watching! That's how I fight, you moron!!

"Come at me yourself," huh?!

I DON'T WANT TO LOSE TO HIM!!

DANG IT...

...

THIS CRUMMY JERK DOESN'T EVEN THINK OF PEOPLE AS PEOPLE!

MY BODY... WON'T MOVE...

End him, Alfred!!

KRAKL KRAKL KRAKL

Guts alone ain't gonna get you out of this, kid!!

Hey... What's with that look?!

`THAT GUY... HE'S...

SHUF

SHUF

...JUST LIKE THAT?!

HE TURNED MY ALFRED INTO CHARCOAL...

...!!

MY APOLOGIES FOR HORNING IN ON YOUR FIGHT.

TUMP

TOTTER

I COULDN'T... BEAT HIM...

DANG IT...

I THOUGHT IT WOULD BE A SHAME TO LET A MAN LIKE YOU DIE HERE.

FORGIVE ME!

I HATE TO ADMIT IT, BUT IT LOOKS AS THOUGH YAMI'S FORESIGHT WAS BETTER THAN MINE.

EVEN WITH VERY LITTLE MAGIC POWER, ONE SHOULD BE ABLE TO FLOAT A LITTLE.

WHAT'S GOING ON?

YOU'RE A PEASANT, WITH NO MAGIC.

I'M IMPRESSED YOU FOUGHT THIS FAR.

OKAY, HE'S TOTALLY NO GOOD!

WHY IS HE EVEN HERE?!

WHAT THE HECK, MAN? THAT TWERP'S UNBELIEVABLE!

THIS GUY IS...

THE CAPTAIN OF THE CRIMSON LION KING MAGIC KNIGHTS...

I GET IT... THIS GUY'S...

FUEGOLEON...

FOOM

LEAVE THE REST TO ME!!

....VERMILLION!!!

Charmy
Pappitson

Age: 19
Height: 142 cm
Birthday: June 3
Sign: Gemini
Blood Type: A
Likes: **Food**

❈ Page 31: The Crimson Lion King

"...ARE RIVALS AS WELL."

"THEN YOU AND I...

...JUST CALL ME HIS...?!

DID A MAGIC KNIGHT CAPTAIN...

YOUR EXUBERANCE MAY BE YOUR GREATEST WEAPON, BUT KEEP A COOL HEAD AS WELL!

WARRIORS MUST MONITOR THEIR OWN CONDITION, CONSTANTLY DETERMINING WHETHER OR NOT THEY CAN FIGHT.

WOORGH

DRIP DRIP

IF YOU REALLY INTEND TO BECOME THE WIZARD KING, THAT IS.

AT THIS POINT, YOU'RE IN NO SHAPE FOR IT!

YOUR ACTIONS ARE TOO SCATTERED FOR AN INVASION AND TOO ORGANIZED FOR INDISCRIMINATE TERRORISM.

WHO ARE YOU?!

WHAT IS IT THAT YOU PEOPLE WANT?!

HAH
...!

...

...I WAS THE TOP CHOICE FOR A MAGIC KNIGHT SQUAD. THE NAME'S RADES.

SIX YEARS AGO...

HE'S A COMMONER, BUT THE STRENGTH OF HIS MAGIC IS PHENOMENAL!

...!!

AH...

...! WHAT ?!

A FORMER MAGIC KNIGHT?!

I WASN'T IMPORTANT ENOUGH FOR YOU PEOPLE TO BOTHER WITH.

YOU DON'T REMEMBER, DO YOU?

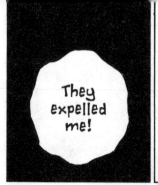

They expelled me!

WITH ALL THAT TALENT, WHY WOULD YOU...?!

THAT MAN...?! AS I RECALL, HE JOINED THE PURPLE ORCAS...

So that's why!! I'm avenging myself against those Magic Knights and the country!!

With this power!!

That's why I'm doing this!!!

ALTHOUGH, YEAH, THERE'S ONE OTHER REASON...!

They said my wraith magic was dangerous, forbidden...

Since I was a commoner, nobody had my back. They exiled me from both the Knights and the country!!

Wasn't magic supposed to be everything?! Huh?!

Better than the nobles... Better than anyone!!

Even though my talents were better...

DO YOU NEED HELP?!

IF YOU UNDERSTAND WHAT YOU NEED TO DO, THEN GET IT DONE QUICK!!

THAT'S WHAT I LIKE TO HEAR!!

DEFINITELY NOT!!

...

Well, it's not like I'd let you go save him anyway...

HA HA HA HA

The affinity between their attributes is lousy!

Way to ask the impossible!!

WH... WHOOOAA... SPARTAN BROTHERS!!

GONG

SORRY, I'M NOT GOING TO BE ABLE TO CONTROL THE INTENSITY OF THIS FLAME.

Flame Creation Magic: Leorzenas

HWOOOOO

SWOOOOOOSH

KEH
HEH
HEH

FOOOON

WHEN HE WAS ALIVE, THIS GUY WAS A DEFENSE MAGIC EXPERT.

NUMBER ONE, CARL.

I ADDED MY CURSE MAGIC TO THAT AND MADE HIM EVEN TOUGHER TO GET PAST!!

DO YOU REMEMBER WHAT I SAID A MOMENT AGO?

ASTA.

HE'S BRINGING OUT THINGS LIKE THAT AGAIN...!

...

What're you acting all calm for?!

This guy does more than just defend!!

WATCH CAREFULLY!

Flame
Creation
Magic:

Ignis
Columna

Trying to match barrier spells with Carl, huh?!

FWOOOSH

I CERTAINLY CAN'T TOUCH YOU...

Whaddaya think of this iron defense plus super barrage ?!

How's this?!

Mister Captain of the Crimson Lions!!

Ha ha ha ha! Is that all you got?!

...SOL LINEA!

FLAME MAGIC...

!!

I MEET WITH DIFFICULT MAGIC EVERY DAY.

...FOR JUST A MOMENT, THE MANA OF THE BARRIER THINS IN PLACES. I AIMED FOR THAT.

IN THE INSTANT YOU ATTACK...

LISTEN WELL!!

WHEN IT HAPPENS, IF YOU GAUGE THE ABILITY CALMLY AND MAINTAIN A BOLD FIGHTING SPIRIT, YOU WILL NEVER LOSE!!

BECAUSE YOU ARE MAGIC KNIGHTS, YOU WILL FIND YOURSELVES CONSTANTLY PITTED AGAINST POWERFUL ENEMIES AND MAGIC.

KRAK
KRAK
THAT'S MY BIG BROTHER FOR YOU!!

IS THAT CLEAR?!

FOOM

YES, SIR!!!

CAN'T BE WASTING TIME ON A GUY LIKE THIS!

FIDGET

SO THAT'S A MAGIC KNIGHTS CAPTAIN!!

FIDGET

MAN... HE'S AWESOME!!!

...

HE SAW THE WEAKNESS IN THAT ONE INSTANT...

...AND HE EVEN PSYCHED UP HIS ALLIES...

Fuegoleon Vermillion

Age: 30   Height: 188 cm
Birthday: August 5   Sign: Leo   Blood Type: A
Likes: People who want to improve, long soaks in large public baths

Character   Profile

THAT'S THE SPIRIT! WELL DONE!!

THAT'S WHAT QUALIFIES YOU TO LEAD THIS COUNTRY AS ROYALS!!

WE TOOK ADVANTAGE OF THE GAPS IN THE ENEMY'S MANA AND EVAPORATED IT WITH INTENSE FIREPOWER!!

I got caught up in the moment and actually saluted!

VWIP

YES, SIR!!

I...

I'VE GOT JUST AS MUCH MAGIC AS A ROYAL!!

IT CAN'T BE...

THAT CAN'T BE...

Leo Palma!!

Flame-Binding Magic:

WHR OOSH

SHF

!

BEFORE I DO, I'M GOING TO CONFISCATE YOUR GRIMOIRE.

THERE ARE MANY, MANY THINGS I WANT TO ASK YOU!

SHUF

SHUF

SHUF

O O O

Let me go, you piece of—!!

I'm still...

THIS GRIMOIRE...

SHUF

!

Get your hands off my grimoire!

NOOOOOO!!

TUG

THAT'S IT.

WHAT IS THIS?! THE GRIMOIRE...

IT ONLY HAS ONE PAGE?!

THIS GUY... CAN ONLY USE ONE SPELL?!

Give it back!!

Don't look!!

Quit looking!!!

...look down on me!!

Don't you dare...

Couldn't you have made people acknowledge you some other way?

TOK TOK

!

Who'd look down on you?!

WHAT A WASTE!!

EVEN THOUGH YOU'VE GOT THAT AWESOME MAGIC...

EVEN THOUGH YOU HAVE SO MUCH POWER...

HEH

...

...WAS A JUST HEART!

YOU WERE ABLE TO OVERCOME ADVERSITY, BUT WHAT YOU LACKED...

SHUF

...FOR YOUR CRIMES!

PAY...

GRIT

SATISFIED NOW, I TRUST.

YOU'RE...

THERE WILL BE NO MORE ARBITRARY ACTIONS.

MY MAGIC IS ALSO VERY NEAR ITS LIMIT.

SOMETIMES YOU CAN'T WIN, EVEN WITH ENORMOUS MAGIC. CATHERINE WAS CARELESS AND LOST AS WELL.

AS I THOUGHT... DEFEATING A CAPTAIN WAS TOO MUCH TO ASK OF YOUR POWER ALONE.

FOR THE MASTER'S SAKE...

STARTING NOW, WE'LL MOVE ACCORDING TO PLAN.

...?

A VOICE...?

TWITCH

OUR REAL OBJECTIVE IS...

KEH HEH HEH HEH HEH

EVEN IF YOUR OBJECTIVE WAS REVENGE... WHAT IS YOUR GROUP'S OBJECTIVE?!

AT THE VERY LEAST, ONE MORE— A SPATIAL-MAGIC USER— HAS INVADED THE CAPITAL. WHERE ARE THEY?!

DID THEY RUN ALREADY?

FUEGO-LEON VER-MILLION!

YOU!!

WHAT ...?!

!

CRUMB

THIS IS...

SPATIAL MAGIC!!

FINE.

NOTHING VENTURED...

BLORP

BIG BROTH-ER!!!

WHAT IS THIS PLACE...?!

YOU'RE ...!

WHERE DID YOU SEND MY BROTHER ?!!

HA HA HA HA HA

YOU FREAK !!!

SO WHERE ...?!

THAT SUPER-ACCURATE SPATIAL MAGIC... THE USER COULD NEVER HAVE DONE IT. IF THEY WEREN'T NEARBY!

LEO!! THAT MAN ISN'T A SPATIAL-MAGIC USER!

HA HA HA HA HA

WHAT'S SO FUNNY ?!

GOOD JOB SEEING THROUGH THAT.

...!

HE WAS MIXED IN WITH THEM?!

YOU'RE LIKE A WILD ANIMAL, BOY.

...SO I WENT TO THE TROUBLE OF WEARING THIS FILTHY DISGUISE. AND YET...

I FIGURED IF I DISGUISED MYSELF WITH MAGIC, MAGIC COULD FIND ME OUT...

FUE...

...

Leopold
Vermillion

Age: 16   Height: 164 cm
Birthday: August 13   Sign: Leo   Blood Type: O
Likes: Interesting guys, his big brother

C h a r a c t e r   P r o f i l e

HE WAS...
HE WAS SO STRONG, AND THEY JUST...

IT CAN'T BE...

Ghk .....!!

FUEGO-
LEON...

HIS
ARM
...!!

FUEGOLEON!!!

FUEGOLEON

THIS CAN'T BE REAL.

MY BROTHER... WOULDN'T...

...!!

MY BROTHER... WOULDN'T LOSE. THERE'S NO WAY...

IF THE GRIMOIRE'S STILL WHOLE, THEN...

THUMP !

CAPTAIN FUEGOLEON'S...

...GRIMOIRE!!

PATE PATE !!

NO...! THE GRIMOIRE'S STARTING TO CRUMBLE!

IF ONLY MIMOSA WERE HERE ...!!

HE'S STILL ALIVE!!

WE HAVE TO STOP THE BLEEDING !!

Remember when you mouthed off to me a minute ago?!

AA A A

LEOPOLD!! HELP ME!

MUTTER MUTTER

IT CAN'T BE... FUEGO-LEON...

BOOM!!

...

A MAGIC BLAST!!

LEOPOLD!!

A JUST HEART, HUH?!

SHUFF

"YOU WERE ABLE TO OVERCOME ADVERSITY, WHAT YOU LACKED..."

"...WAS A JUST HEART!"

Go yap your head off in the next world, Fuegoleon Vermillion!!

I always do **just** what my heart tells me to!!

WE'VE DONE WHAT WE CAME TO DO.

LET'S GO, RADES. BEFORE ANY OTHER MAGIC KNIGHTS SHOW UP.

YOUR NAME WAS ASTA, YEAH?

!

STAGGER

HOLD IT... RIGHT THERE!!

Look forward to it, you little punk!!

Well, I'll kill you and make you into one of my toys real soon!!

GRRAAAAAAAAH!!

THE WAY HE'S BLEEDING, IF HE MOVES AROUND MUCH MORE...

ASTA...! IT'S NO GOOD!

IT'S TOO FAR... I'M NOT GONNA MAKE IT!

...

...TO STOP THAT GUY?!

WHAT CAN I DO...

IT'S JUST LIKE THE CRIMSON CAPTAIN SAID.

CALM DOWN... AND THINK!!

I'M NOT DONE YET!!!

OH!

THAT SPATIAL MAGIC...

THIS SWORD IS...

WHAT THE...

ANTI-MAGIC!!!

NOT GOOD.

Whaddaya think you're doing, trash?!

YAAAAAGH!!

OWWWWWWW!!

AFTER YOU HURT ALL THOSE PEOPLE...?

HOW...

...DARE YOU!!

SPL AK

I'M HERE TO MAKE SURE THAT DOESN'T HAPPEN!!!

...

...THAT EVEN PEOPLE WITH NO MAGIC CAN BE THE STRONGEST!!!

AND... I'LL BECOME THE WIZARD KING AND PROVE...

ANTI-MAGIC...
IT'S MORE OF A NUISANCE THAN I IMAGINED.

IF I COULD, I'D BE DOING IT.

VALTOS!!

DO SOMETHING!!

HE'S STORING UP MAGIC...

?!

NJINNK

FWIIII

IT SEEMS WE'LL HAVE TO TAKE CARE OF THE BOY FIRST.

IS HE PLANNING TO ATTACK THROUGH HIS SPATIAL MAGIC?!

!

ZUM

FIVE OF THEM...!!

REINFORCE-MENTS?!

...PIERCING COLD MAGIC!!

WHAT...

AGAINST PEOPLE LIKE THESE...? PITIFUL.

WE RECEIVED A REPORT FROM *OUR MASTER* AND CAME, BUT...

ZA

Still... looks like the tables just turned!!

Tch!!

BADMP
BADMP
BADMP

BECAUSE OF THAT CURSE POWER, EVEN THOUGH THEY'RE JUST SCRATCHES, THEY WON'T STOP BLEEDING.

IF I LOSE MUCH MORE BLOOD... THINGS COULD GET UGLY.

HEH
...

HEH
HEH
HEH
...

NOW...

!!

WATCH
ME,
SIR!!

...I
CAN KEEP
FIGHTING!!

THAT GUY... HE HIT HIMSELF WITH HIS OWN BLADES AND TOOK OUT THE CURSE POWER!!

...

I'VE LIVED WITH *ADVERSITY* SINCE I WAS BORN.

Y'KNOW WHAT?

...I'LL BLAST THEM ALL AWAY!!!

NO MATTER WHAT HAPPENS OR HOW MANY PEOPLE COME AT ME...

The Blank Page Brigade

This volume's topic:
What lines in the
manga made the biggest
impression on you?
(A reader submitted this topic!)

"I'll protect you...!" by Noelle

Genya Hori

"I'm not done yet...!!!" by Asta

Masayoshi Satoshō

"Surpass your limits. Right here. Right now." by Yami

Asahi Sakano

I'm a **really** bad loser!!

"I'm a **really** bad loser!!" by Yuno

Teruaki Mizuno

"Being weak is nothing to be ashamed of. *Staying weak* is!!" by Fuegoleon

Kō Shimameguri

"I could not be any more reluctant." by Sandler

...any more reluctant!!

Kōki Ishikawa

"Don't look!!" by Rades

DON'T LOOK!!

Hayato Gotō

...

MISTER MAGIC KNIGHT!

WHROOSH

WHAT ON EARTH IS HAPPENING...?

BRING IT ON!!

AWRIGHT!

✿ Page 34: Wounded Beasts

YOUR
STRUGGLES
ARE
POINTLESS
...

THE
ANTI-MAGIC
KID THE
MASTER WAS
TALKING
ABOUT!

HEH
HEH
HEH

OH...
IT'S
HIM.

STAY CALM.

RIGHT.

HUFF

HUFF

YOUR EXUBERANCE MAY BE YOUR GREATEST WEAPON, BUT KEEP A COOL HEAD AS WELL!

RRAAAAH!

I'M GONNA CALMLY...

...KICK YOUR BUTTS!!

THAT LITTLE ...!

Flame Magic:
Exploding Flames

YOU THINK I'M GOING TO LET YOU PEOPLE THROW YOUR WEIGHT AROUND...

...AFTER WHAT YOU DID TO MY BROTHER?!

LET ME JOIN YOU, MY RIVAL!!

SURE, JUMP RIGHT ON IN!

THEY SAY BEASTS ARE MORE FORMIDABLE WHEN WOUNDED.

THESE BOYS ARE...

...DANGEROUS.

...WE'LL KILL YOU HERE AND NOW!!

YOU WEREN'T OUR TARGETS, BUT...

Water Creation Magic: Sea Dragon's Lair!!

FOOOOM !! SZZAP OOOOM SZZAP SZZAP

WELL, WELL.

THAT'S QUITE A NICE BARRIER SPELL!

DON'T THINK YOU CAN KILL MY FRIENDS SO EASILY!!

KRAK KRAK

IN THAT CASE, I'LL OPPOSE YOU WITH GRIMOIRE MAGIC. I WOULDN'T WANT TO BE RUDE.

FLIP

FROM YOUR APPEARANCE, YOU'RE A MEMBER OF THE ROYAL SILVA FAMILY, CORRECT?

Tree
Creation
Magic:
Magic-
Draining
Roots

RUSTLE
RUSTLE RUSTLE

ZZT
ZZT

ZLURK
ZLURK
ZLURK

ZZT ZZT ZZT ZZT

YOUR
FIGHTING
INSTINCTS
ARE
ADMIRABLE.

FLIP
FLAP

BA
RAAA!!!
BAH

!!

SLUURK
SLUURK

!!!

NO
WAY...!!
THEY
SWALLOWED
THAT
TORRENT?!

BLUFF

Wind Creation Magic:

Tornado Needles

THOOOOO!!

HE'S TOO FAST...!!

...

HE:...

NO... NO WAY...!!

LET'S FINISH THEM OFF, SHALL WE?

NOW THEN...

VVUM

THUD

THIS
MAGIC...
IT'S...!

WHAT
...?

MAGIC KNIGHTS!

Y... YOU GUYS...!

IMPOS-
SIBLE...!

YOU
COVERED
THAT
DISTANCE
THIS
QUICKLY?!

!

HOW DARE
YOU SEND US
ALL THE WAY
OUT THERE?!

WE REALLY DIDN'T WANT TO...BUT WE ALL WORKED TOGETHER TO GET BACK.

I SUPPOSE I SHOULD CALL IT SUPER COMPOUND MAGIC.

WE REALLY DON'T PLAY WELL WITH OTHERS, YOU KNOW.

TCH!

I'M NEVER COOPERATING AGAIN.

HMPH

I'LL ACKNOWLEDGE THEIR ABILITIES. NO MORE.

WELL, I GUESS MEN AREN'T TOTALLY USELESS.

JOINING FORCES ISN'T BAD, IS IT!

Oh ho ho ho!

...

SKRATCH SKRATCH

...EXIST TO PROTECT THE PEACE OF THE ONE CLOVER KINGDOM!!

HOWEVER... OUR NINE MAGIC KNIGHT SQUADS...

IT'LL COST US IF WE KEEP FIGHTING. LET'S RETREAT.

TCH...

Mercury Magic: Rain of Silver

WHAT'S THE RUSH?

SHUF

WHAT...

BAH

...IS THAT MAGIC ITEM?!

AB H

AND THEN...

MY RAIN WILL GO RIGHT THROUGH A SPELL LIKE THAT.

R

GATOOMP

GUP

ASTA!

WE ARE THE *EYE OF THE MIDNIGHT SUN.*

WHAT ARE YOU GOING TO DO WITH HIM?

HEH HEH HEH HEH ♪ THAT'S A SECRET.

BLOOP

M·I·I·NE!

ASTA ....!!

ASTA !!

THEY JUST DEFLECTED A CAPTAIN'S SPELL AS IF IT WAS NOTHING!!

...MAGIC KNIGHTS.

REMEMBER THIS...

Special Support Manga from Yuto Tsukuda: "Memories with Tabacchan"

I went to help Tabata finish up a one-shot for the Gold Future Cup.

Summer 2011.

BESIDES, TSUKU-TSUKU (NICKNAME), YOU'VE HAD EXPERIENCE WORKING ON SERIALS WITH *SHONEN DASH* (TSUKUDA'S OLD SERIES), SO IT WOULD BE GREAT IF YOU COULD LOOK OVER THE OVERALL SCHEDULE FOR ME TOO.

NO, THAT'LL BE A HUGE HELP!

Excuse the intrusion.

ALL I CAN DO IS COLOR IN SOLID AREAS AND LAY DOWN SIMPLE TONE...

?

HUH...? I DUNNO.

?!

AND? ABOUT HOW MANY PAGES ARE ALMOST DONE?

AH, I SEE. SURE! THE DEADLINE'S COMING UP FAST, AFTER ALL.

NOM NOM

AREN'T YOU GONNA EAT, TSUKU-TSUKU?

I'm glad we made it!

Watching out of the corner of his eye, Tabacchan started chowing down on a takeout bento.

Realizing that even with the deadline only a few days away, no one knew how far they were on the manuscript, Tsukuda went pale and hurried to check.

Congrats on the release of *Black Clover* volume 4!! As a reader, I always enjoy the incredible art and composition skills, and the protagonist Asta's straightforward enthusiasm.

Back when I lived in Tabata's neighborhood, we'd meet at the pub night after night and talk about manga for hours on end. Those are terrific memories. Now we both have manga running in the same magazine, and I feel like, "We did it! Go, us!"

Let's both keep giving it our best!!

Tsukuday-to

Food Wars!: Shokugeki no Soma, written by Yuto Tsukuda, currently runs in *Weekly Shonen Jump* and is available as graphic novels!

This volume's topic: What lines in the manga made the biggest impression on you?

"My magic is never giving up!!!" by Asta

Captain Tabata

Comics Editor Tomiyama

"So that means... You're a real man, ain'tcha!" by Magna

" ... " by Nero

Editor Zenas !!!

Wife Zenas !!!

"I said *no*." by Charmy

FWOOSH
Editor Katayama

FWOOSH
©

AFTERWORD

❀

This time, Tsukuda Sensei a.k.a., my friend Tsuku-Tsuku, drew a support manga for me! Woohoo! Thank yooooou!!

We're from the same part of the country, and he's close to my age. Since he was a nice person with a good head on his shoulders, I had him hang out with me a lot. Heh heh heh.

He's a really nice guy who gave a flawless speech as the representative of my friends at my wedding.

He's really enthusiastic about manga, and at the pub, although I always said insubstantial stuff, the things he said were really useful, and I always used them as reference. Heh heh heh.

I'm seriously moved that I get to work hard in the same magazine with a guy like that!
"We did it! Go, us!"
Come by the studio to work on roughs again, okay?

Special Bonus Materials

Presenting early sketches of the Silva siblings and more! You can see the process of trial and error they went through before they were completed. By the way, who's the character with a striking resemblance to *that* person...??

Noelle Silva

Nozel Silva

Solid Silva

C'mon.

???

Hamon Caseus

Lotus Whomalt

Shiren Tium

NARUTO

Story and Art by
Masashi Kishimoto

Naruto is determined to become the greatest ninja ever!

Twelve years ago the Village Hidden in the Leaves was attacked by a fearsome threat. A nine-tailed fox spirit claimed the life of the village leader, the Hokage, and many others. Today, the village is at peace and a troublemaking kid named Naruto is struggling to graduate from Ninja Academy. His goal may be to become the next Hokage, but his true destiny will be much more complicated. The adventure begins now!

WORLD'S BEST SELLING MANGA!

www.shonenjump.com

www.viz.com

Stop

YOU'RE READING
THE WRONG WAY!

BLACK CLOVER

reads from right to left, starting
in the upper-right corner. Japanese
is read from right to left, meaning
that action, sound effects, and
word-balloon order are completely
reversed from English order.